APR 0 4 2014

j979.4 J68c
California gold rush! /
Johnson, Robin

WITHDRAWN

S0-AWF-509

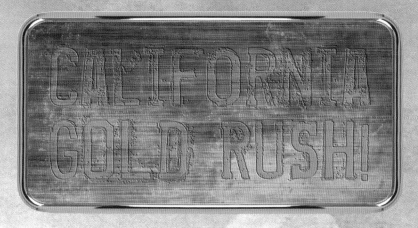

CALIFORNIA GOLD RUSH!

Robin Johnson

CRABTREE
Publishing Company
www.crabtreebooks.com

Crabtree Publishing Company
www.crabtreebooks.com

Author: Robin Johnson
Publishing plan research and development: Reagan Miller
Editor: Kathy Middleton
Proofreader: Shannon Welbourn
Photo Researchers: Robin Johnson, Rachel Minay
Original design: Tim Mayer (Mayer Media)
Book design: Kim Williams (320 Media)
Cover design: Ken Wright
Production coordinator and prepress tecnician: Ken Wright
Print coordinator: Margaret Amy Salter

Produced for Crabtree Publishing Company by White-Thomson Publishing

Photographs:
Corbis: pp. 18–19; Bettmann: pp. 8–9, 11 bottom, 16–17, 34–35; PEMCO – Webster & Stevens Collection; Museum of History and Industry, Seattle: pp. 42–43; PoodlesRock: pp. 12–13; Getty: MCT Graphics via Getty Images: p. 11 top; Library of Congress: pp. 14–15, 24–25, 30–31, 36–37, 37; Shutterstock: Atlaspix: p. 45; catwalker: p. 3; dibrova: p. 4; Hanze: pp. 38–39; Jim Feliciano: pp. 44–45; Shyamalamuralinath: p. 5; SuperStock: pp. 32–33; ClassicStock.com: pp. 26–27; Corbis: pp. 6–7, Huntington Library: pp. 4–5; Image Asset Management Ltd: p. 14; Newberry Library: pp. 22–23, 28–29; Underwood Photo Archives; pp. 40–41; Topfoto: The Granger Collection: p. 20; White-Thomson Publishing/Stefan Chabluk: pp. 6, 10, 21; Wikimedia: p. 1; © Look and Learn/The Bridgeman Art Library: front cover

Library and Archives Canada Cataloguing in Publication

Johnson, Robin (Robin R.), author
    California gold rush! / Robin Johnson.

(Crabtree chrome)
Includes index.
Issued in print and electronic formats.
ISBN 978-0-7787-1170-4 (bound).--ISBN 978-0-7787-1178-0 (pbk.).--ISBN 978-1-4271-8931-8 (pdf).--ISBN 978-1-4271-8923-3 (html)

    1. Gold mines and mining--California--History--19th century--Juvenile literature. 2. Frontier and pioneer life--California--Juvenile literature. 3. California--Gold discoveries--Juvenile literature. 4. California--History--1846-1850--Juvenile literature. I. Title. II. Series: Crabtree chrome

F865.J65 2013   j979.4'04   C2013-905239-9
                                        C2013-905240-2

Library of Congress Cataloging-in-Publication Data

Johnson, Robin (Robin R.)
    California gold rush! / Robin Johnson.
      pages cm. -- (Crabtree chrome)
    Includes index.
    ISBN 978-0-7787-1170-4 (reinforced library binding) --
ISBN 978-0-7787-1178-0 (pbk.) -- ISBN 978-1-4271-8931-8
(electronic pdf) -- ISBN 978-1-4271-8923-3 (electronic html)
    1. California--Gold discoveries--Juvenile literature.
2. California--History--1846-1850--Juvenile literature.
3. Frontier and pioneer life--California--Juvenile literature.
I. Title.

    F865.J65 2013
    979.4'03--dc23
                                    2013030092

Crabtree Publishing Company
www.crabtreebooks.com   1-800-387-7650

Printed in Canada/102013/BF20130920

Copyright © **2014 CRABTREE PUBLISHING COMPANY.** All rights reserved. No part of this publication may be reproduced, stored in a retrieval system or be transmitted in any form or by any means, electronic, mechanical, photocopying, recording, or otherwise, without the prior written permission of Crabtree Publishing Company. In Canada: We acknowledge the financial support of the Government of Canada through the Canada Book Fund for our publishing activities.

Published in Canada
Crabtree Publishing
616 Welland Ave.
St. Catharines, ON
L2M 5V6

Published in the United States
Crabtree Publishing
PMB 59051
350 Fifth Avenue, 59th Floor
New York, New York 10118

Published in the United Kingdom
Crabtree Publishing
Maritime House
Basin Road North, Hove
BN41 1WR

Published in Australia
Crabtree Publishing
3 Charles Street
Coburg North
VIC 3058

Contents

CALIFORNIA GOLD RUSH 1849

USA 33

1999

California Dreams

Going for Gold

On January 24, 1848, carpenter James W. Marshall was standing in a river in California when something shiny caught his eye. Gold! Suddenly, the rush was on. People from around the world came to California by the thousands in ships and wagons. They were determined to find gold and get rich—or die trying.

Gold is a precious metal. It is valuable because there is not a lot of it in the world. In the United States, gold was first found in 1799 in North Carolina. In 1828, more gold was found in Georgia. But the biggest Gold Rush took place in California.

Rich Man, Poor Man

From 1848 to 1855, about 300,000 people took part in the California **Gold Rush**. They worked hard and fought for their fortunes. Some got lucky and struck gold. Many left broke and empty-handed. All had tales to tell of the Wild West and its treasures.

▼ *Used to make coins, jewelry, art, and other treasures, gold has been mined around the world for thousands of years. The picture below shows a gold mine in Taylorsville, California, in 1849—just a year after gold was discovered in the state.*

Gold Rush: when many people hurry to an area that has gold

Wild West

In the 1840s, California was still part of Mexico. It was a huge and wild area of land, home to Mohave, Chumash, Shasta, and many other Native nations. Only a few thousand settlers from Europe had moved there. These early **pioneers** survived by growing crops, raising cattle, and trapping animals for their fur.

▼ *In 1845, California belonged to Mexico. Texas was an independent nation. By 1848, both areas of land would belong to the United States.*

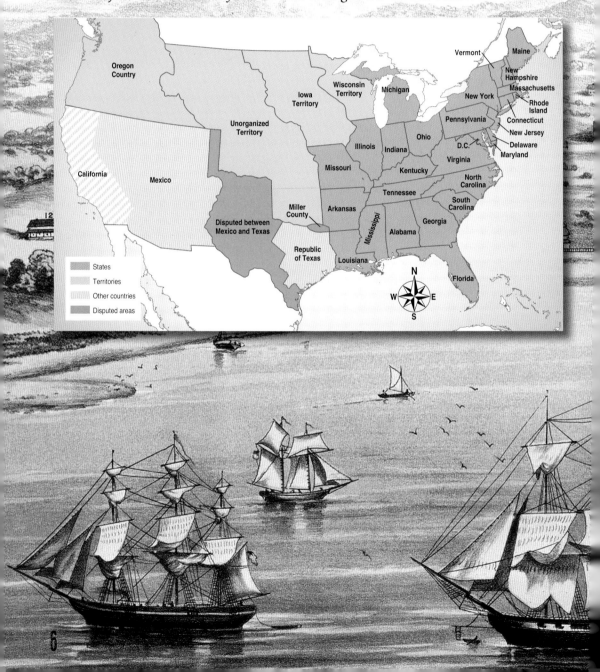

Oregon Country

Iowa Territory

Wisconsin Territory

Michigan

Vermont

Maine

New Hampshire

Massachusetts

New York

Rhode Island

Pennsylvania

Connecticut

New Jersey

Ohio

D.C.

Delaware

Maryland

Unorganized Territory

Illinois

Indiana

Virginia

Missouri

Kentucky

North Carolina

California

Mexico

Tennessee

South Carolina

Miller County

Arkansas

Georgia

Disputed between Mexico and Texas

Alabama

Mississippi

Republic of Texas

Louisiana

Florida

States

Territories

Other countries

Disputed areas

12

6

The Mexican-American War

In 1846, Mexico and the United States began fighting for control of Texas. The Mexican-American War ended on February 2, 1848, with the Treaty of Guadalupe Hidalgo. The treaty gave Texas—and California—to the United States. No one knew that gold had been discovered in California just nine days earlier.

About 150,000 Native people lived in California in the 1840s. Many were driven from their lands or killed during the Gold Rush. Others starved or died from smallpox and other diseases that were brought to California by European settlers.

▼ *The United States wanted California for its port cities, such as San Francisco. The ports would allow American ships to trade goods with Asia.*

pioneers: people who are among the first to live in a new area

7

Sutter's Mill

Some early settlers built mills along California rivers. They used the mills to make flour, lumber, or other goods. In 1847, John A. Sutter decided to start a **sawmill** in Coloma, California. He hired James W. Marshall to build it.

Marshall's Discovery

One day, Marshall was standing in the American River inspecting the sawmill. He noticed some yellow flakes shining in the water. Marshall scooped up four or five pieces to get a closer look. He could not believe his eyes. His heart began to race. Could it be gold?

◀ *John A. Sutter planned to make his fortune by making lumber for settlers.*

> **"It made my heart thump, for I was certain it was gold."**
>
> James W. Marshall

sawmill: a building where logs are cut into boards

Gold Fever!

Hidden Treasure

Marshall and Sutter had the metal tested to see if it was really gold. They were amazed to find out that it was! The two men tried to keep their discovery a secret, but word soon spread. They could not even finish building their sawmill— all the workers had left to hunt for gold!

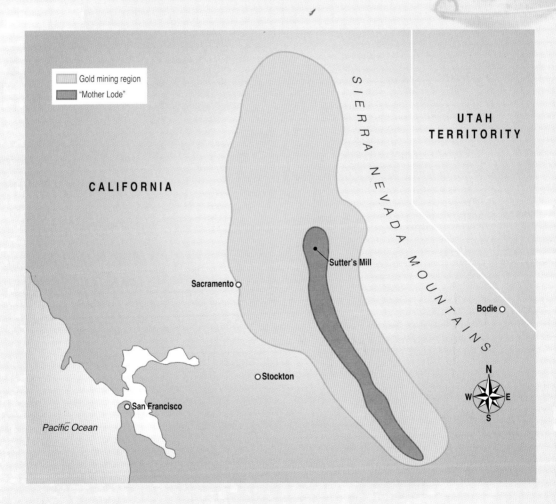

▲ *Hopeful miners flocked to mines that sprang up throughout California. Many of the mines were in the California Mother Lode—an area of land that was rich in gold.*

Good News

News of the gold soon reached the nearby town of San Francisco. Samuel Brannan rode through the streets of the town waving a little bottle of gold dust for all to see. Brannan was a **merchant** who was eager to sell supplies to miners.

▶ *Brannan made so much money selling mining supplies that he was called the richest man in California.*

GOOD NEWS

FOR

MINERS.

NEW GOODS,

PROVISIONS, TOOLS,

CLOTHING, &c. &c.

GREAT BARGAINS!

JUST RECEIVED BY THE SUBSCRIBERS, AT THE LARGE TENT ON THE HILL,

A superior Lot of New, Valuable and most DESIRABLE GOODS for Miners and for residents also. Among them are the following:

STAPLE PROVISIONS AND STORES.

Pork, Flour, Bread, Beef, Hams, Mackerel, Sugar, Molasses, Coffee, Teas, Butter & Cheese, Pickles, Beans, Peas, Rice, Chocolate, Spices, Salt, Soap, Vinegar, &c.

EXTRA PROVISIONS AND STORES.

Every variety of Preserved Meats and Vegetables and Fruits, (more than eighty different kinds.) Tongues and Sounds; Smoked Halibut; Dry Cod Fish; Eggs fresh and fine; Figs, Raisins, Almonds and Nuts; China Preserves; China Bread and Cakes; Butter Crackers, Boston Crackers, and many other very desirable and choice bits.

DESIRABLE GOODS FOR COMFORT. AND HEALTH.

Patent Cot Bedsteads, Mattresses and Pillows, Blankets and Comforters. Also, in Clothing—Overcoats, Jackets, Miner's heavy Velvet Coats and Pantaloons, Wooden Pants, Guernsey Frocks, Flannel Shirts and Drawers, Stockings and Socks, Boots, Shoes; Rubber Waders, Coats, Blankets, &c.

MINING TOOLS, &c.; BUILDING MATERIALS, &c.

Cradles, Shovels, Spades, Hoes, Picks, Axes, Hatchets, Hammers; every variety of Workman's Tools, Nails, Screws, Brads, &c.

SUPERIOR GOLD SCALES.   MEDICINE CHESTS, &c.

Superior Medicine Chests, well assorted, together with the principal Important Medicines for Dysentery, Fever and Fever and Ague, Scurvy, &c.

N.B.–Important Express Arrangement for Miners.

The Subscribers will run an EXPRESS to and from every Steamer, carrying and returning Letters for the Post Office and Expresses to the States. Also, conveying "GOLD DUST" or Parcels to and from the Mines to the Banking House, or the several Expresses for the States, insuring their safety.———The various NEWSPAPERS from the Eastern, Western and Southern States, will also be found on sale at our stores, together with a large stock of BOOKS and PAMPHLETS constantly on hand.

Excelsior Tent, Mormon Island, }
January 1, 1850.   }   ALTA CALIFORNIA PRESS

WARREN & CO.

From Original   Courtesy of Bancroft Library

148. Mormon Island Emporium, Excelsior Tent

> "Gold! Gold! Gold! Gold from the American River!"
>
> Merchant Samuel Brannan

◀ *The California Gold Rush was good news for merchants! They sold tools, clothes, and many other goods at high prices.*

 **merchant:** a person who sells goods to make money

Gold Fever

Before long, everyone had gold fever! "Gold fever" is a strong desire to get rich quick and rush to a place that has gold. **Prospectors** raced from San Francisco, hoping to find the precious metal and make their fortunes. People from the rest of California were not far behind them.

"**The discovery of ... gold has entirely changed ... California. Its people, before engaged in [growing] their small patches of ground, and guarding their herds of cattle and horses, have all gone to the mines, or are on their way.**"

U.S. Colonel Richard Barnes Mason, 1848

▲ *This illustration shows how miners were willing to fight for a piece of California and the chance to make a fortune.*

Packing Up

Families quickly packed their belongings. They bought the supplies they needed and hurried to the gold fields together. They left their jobs, homes, and farms behind. Across California, crops were left to die in the fields untended. Mills came to a sudden stop.

prospectors: people who search for valuable minerals

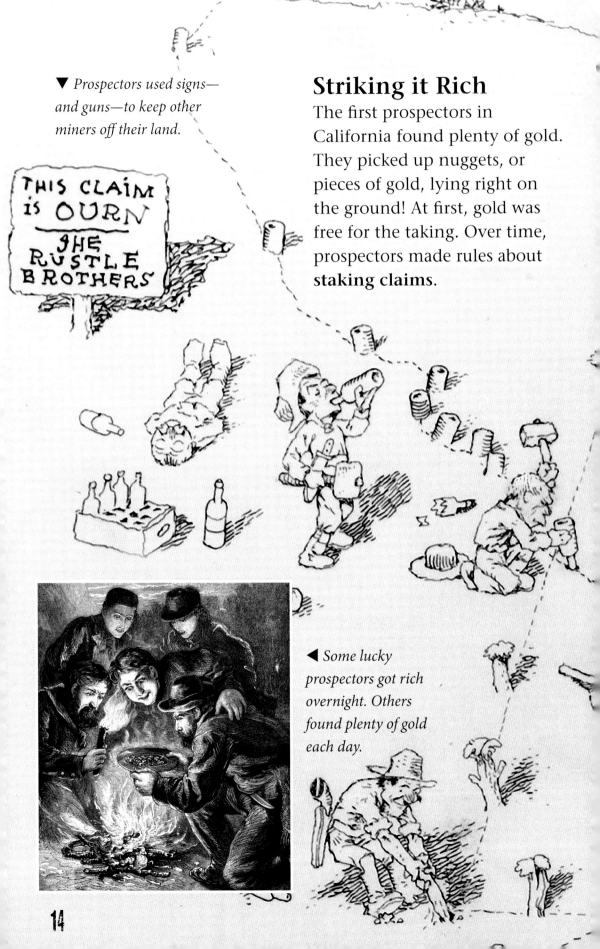

▼ *Prospectors used signs—and guns—to keep other miners off their land.*

THIS CLAIM
is OURN
THE
RUSTLE
BROTHERS

Striking it Rich

The first prospectors in California found plenty of gold. They picked up nuggets, or pieces of gold, lying right on the ground! At first, gold was free for the taking. Over time, prospectors made rules about **staking claims.**

◀ *Some lucky prospectors got rich overnight. Others found plenty of gold each day.*

Staking Claims

When prospectors found gold, they drove wooden posts called stakes into the ground. The stakes showed that the prospectors owned the land and its gold. Prospectors could claim only as much land as they could work. If they stopped mining the land, other prospectors could "claim-jump" and take it over.

When the Gold Rush began, there was no government and no laws in California. Prospectors made their own rules and used guns to keep the peace.

staking claims: using posts to show who owns a piece of land

From Far Away

News of the gold soon spread beyond California. Other hopeful prospectors began arriving by ship. Thousands of **immigrants** came from the Oregon Territory, Hawaii, Mexico, Peru, Chile, and China. Prospectors from Europe and Australia arrived soon after them.

"A company of Chinese have been building a log cabin near us for several days past ... I like to talk with them, and ask them hundreds of questions about their native land ..."

American prospector Timothy Coffin Osborn in 1850

Shared Dream

People came from different lands and had different ways of life. They spoke different languages and wore different clothes. The immigrants all had one thing in common, however. They all shared the dream of finding gold in California.

▼ *Thousands of men came from China looking for work—and gold.*

immigrants: people who go to live in a new country

Wild West Tales

People in the eastern United States began to hear wild tales of California, too. Rivers were flowing with gold! Prospectors were finding gold nuggets the size of plums! Americans were eager to make new homes—and fortunes—in the west. But they were afraid it was too good to be true.

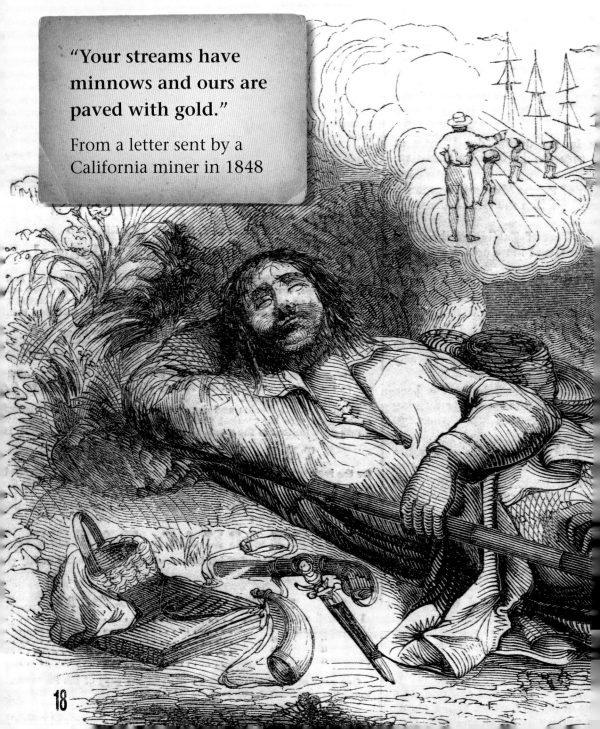

"Your streams have minnows and ours are paved with gold."

From a letter sent by a California miner in 1848

Polk's Speech

In December 1848, U.S. president James Polk gave an important speech. He told Americans about the gold in California and **urged** them to settle there. Polk wanted to expand the territory of the United States west to the Pacific Ocean. He dreamed of a great country that stretched from coast to coast.

▼ *This prospector has big dreams of going west and making a fortune in California.*

urged: tried hard to convince someone to do something

Leaving Home

After Polk's speech, tens of thousands of men hurried to California from across America. Most were farmers who wanted to grow their fortunes fast. They borrowed money or spent their life savings to pay for their trips. These prospectors became known as "49ers" because so many of them arrived in California in 1849.

> *"'Tis true, like others, I may die,*
> *Or you may not live to see me;*
> *But Gold is sparking in my eye,*
> *I am bound for California."*

Part of an 1849 song called "The Gold Hunter's Farewell to his Wife"

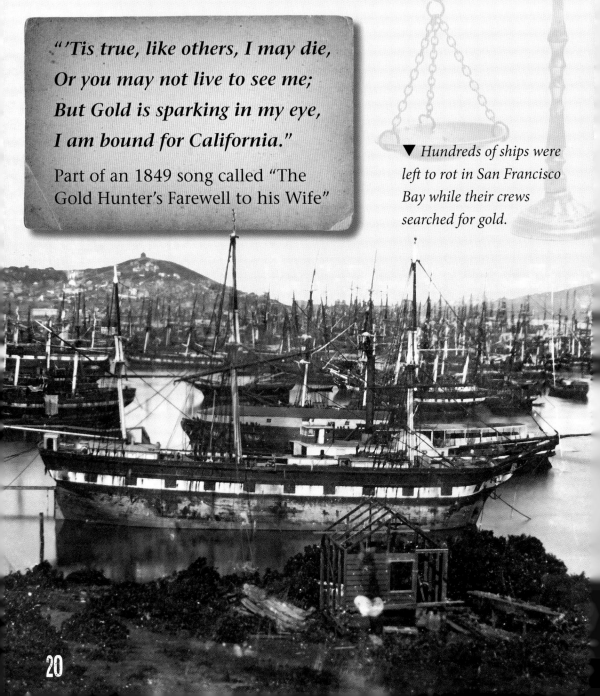

▼ *Hundreds of ships were left to rot in San Francisco Bay while their crews searched for gold.*

Danger at Sea

Many Americans traveled by ship to California. The journey from the east coast was long and dangerous. It took five to eight months to sail down the Atlantic coast and all the way around the tip of South America. Many people died in **shipwrecks** or from diseases at sea. Some people got off in Panama and cut through the jungle to the Pacific Ocean.

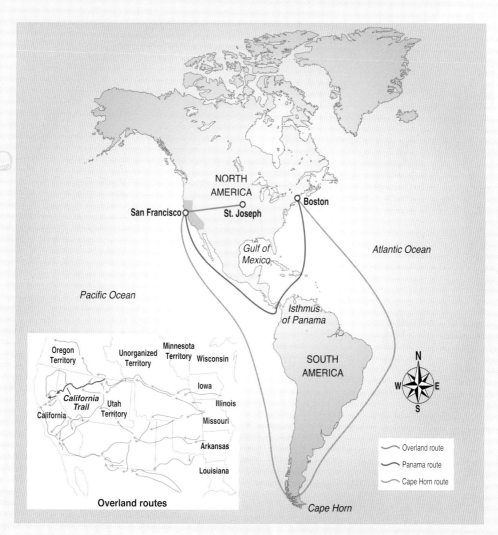

▲ *This map shows the three main routes to California. There were different overland routes, but many people started near St Joseph, Missouri.*

shipwrecks: ships that have crashed or been destroyed at sea

Wagons West

Many pioneers traveled across the United States in covered wagons. They rolled and bumped their way slowly west on the California Trail and other overland routes (see map on page 21). They traveled through dusty prairies, rushing rivers, high mountains, and dry deserts in their pursuit of gold.

▼ *Pioneers loaded food, pots, clothes, blankets, guns, and other supplies into the wagons before they began their long journeys west.*

Danger Trails

The pioneers faced many dangers along the way. Many died from wagon accidents, bad weather, or attacks by Native people as they passed through their lands. Others got sick from diseases such as typhoid or cholera, or starved to death. Pioneers often traveled together for safety from attack. They formed long lines called wagon trains.

"The road was lined with the skeletons of the poor beasts who had died in the struggle. Sometimes we found the bones of men bleaching beside their broken-down and **abandoned** wagons."

Luzena Wilson, one of the few women who went to California during the Gold Rush

abandoned: left behind

Gold Diggers

Hard Labor

Life did not get easier for the pioneers once they reached California. Men spent long days doing backbreaking work in the gold fields. They moved heavy rocks, dug and carried buckets of dirt, and **waded** through icy water up to their waists. Many men got sick or injured on the job.

▶ *Prospectors used sharp picks to break rocks. They used shovels to dig in the ground. They used flat, round metal pans to study small rocks in streams.*

Tools of the Trade

Prospectors carried big, heavy tools with them each day. They used picks, shovels, and pans to find gold. Most prospectors also carried guns to protect themselves. Men were often shot and killed for their gold.

"I have worked harder here than I ever worked at home. I have been repeatedly disappointed in making the amount of money I expected to make here."

Prospector Horace Root, 1851

waded: walked through water

25

Panning for Gold

Most prospectors **panned** for gold. They waded into rivers or crouched beside streams. The miners used their pans to scoop up stones from the water. They gently shook the pans until the water and lighter stones fell out. Then they looked in the pans for gold.

"The day was intensely hot, yet about 200 men were at work in the full glare of the sun, washing for gold ... "

U.S. Colonel Richard Barnes Mason, August 17, 1848

▼ Groups of miners built long wooden channels to move the water from rivers and streams. They moved the water so they could search for gold in dry riverbeds.

Rocking the Cradle

Over time, prospectors found better and faster ways to mine gold. Some built wooden machines called cradles. A cradle was a big box on rockers. Prospectors poured soil into the box. Then they washed out the dirt and—if they were lucky—left gold behind.

panned: used a shallow bowl to separate gold from stones

Give Me Shelter

At the end of the day, weary prospectors returned to their camps. Some people lived in simple log cabins or shacks. Others slept in tents near the gold fields. Many prospectors had no **shelter** at all. They made fires and spread their blankets on the cold, hard ground.

> "There were not roofs enough in the country to shelter the thousands who had arrived by sea and by land."
>
> U.S. General William T. Sherman

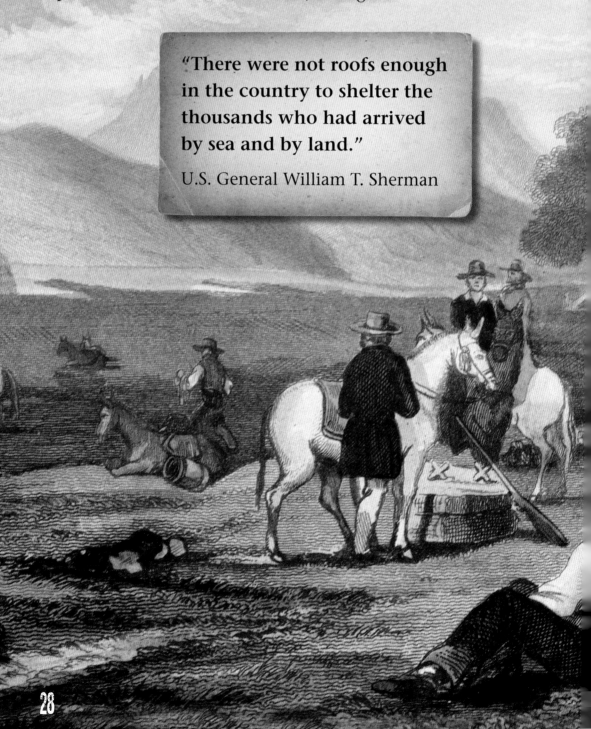

No Comforts

Everyone missed the comforts of home they had left behind. To keep loneliness at bay, as well as soothe their aching muscles and empty bellies, the prospectors played cards and fiddles and drank whiskey. They shared stories of small nuggets and big fortunes and dreamed of striking it rich.

▼ *Hundreds of mining camps appeared in California during the Gold Rush.*

shelter: a place that gives protection from bad weather

Boomtowns

As more and more people moved west, **boomtowns** sprang up throughout California. San Francisco, Sacramento, and other boomtowns became big, busy places. The streets of the towns were lined with shops, restaurants, and hotels to serve the growing number of prospectors.

Finding Trouble

Prospectors poured into the towns to buy supplies. They also came to celebrate their good luck—or drink their troubles away. Rowdy prospectors filled the taverns and gambling halls of the towns. Gunfights often broke out with no one around to keep order.

▼ *Prospectors came into the towns to drink and play cards.*

"When I first saw Sacramento it ... was a terrifying place. I was frightened. Men were gambling on all sides. They were shooting and cursing and yelling. The noise and uproar were awful."

Frances Anne Van Winkle, who came to California with her family

boomtowns: towns that grow very fast

Rags and Riches

Best Sellers

Many people got rich from the Gold Rush without ever digging for gold. In fact, merchants made more money than prospectors did! Merchants sold mining tools, clothing, food, and many other goods. Prospectors were desperate for supplies and were willing to pay top dollar for them.

▼ *A merchant named Levi Strauss sold clothing, bedding, and other dry goods to miners. He later made a fortune making sturdy work pants called blue jeans in factories like this.*

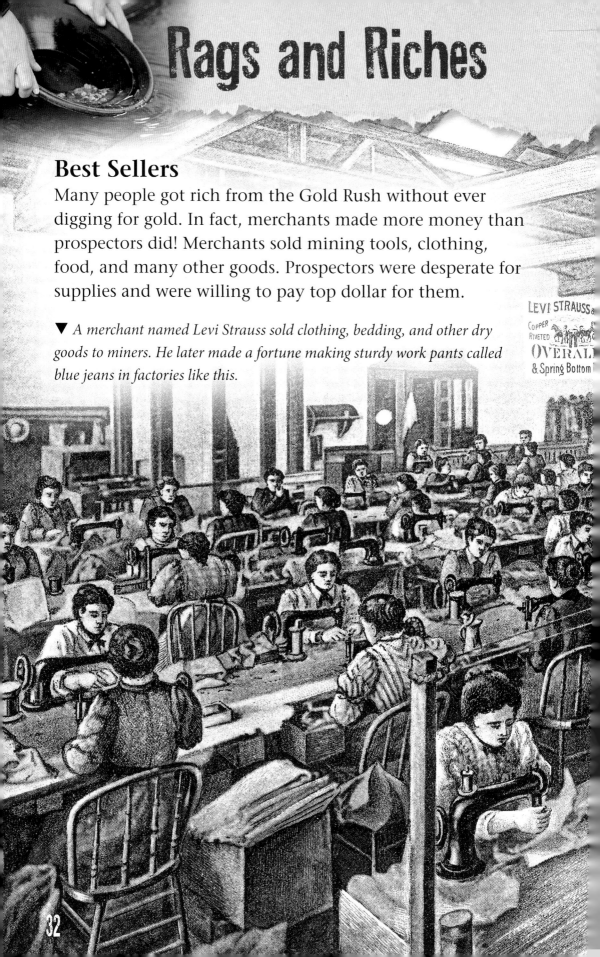

LEVI STRAUSS &
COPPER
RIVETED
OVERALL
& Spring Bottom

Open for Business

People ran all kinds of successful businesses during the Gold Rush. Some people made money by bringing goods and people to California. Others fixed barrels, wagon wheels, guns, and other items. Many women rented rooms to prospectors. Women also sold home-cooked food and ran sewing and laundry businesses.

"I made many an apple pie, just of common dried apples, and sold them for a dollar apiece. The women helped in that way to support the families, for mining was not always a certain means of **livelihood**."

Mrs. Noble Martin

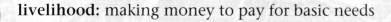

livelihood: making money to pay for basic needs

The Lucky Ones

For some prospectors, the risks and hardships of the California Gold Rush paid off. About half the people who searched for gold made a **profit**. They earned enough to pay for their supplies and take a little money home to their families.

▶ *Prospecting panned out for these lucky gold diggers!*

In the first four years of the Gold Rush, prospectors found more than 200 million dollars' worth of gold. In today's money, that would be about 6 billion dollars! After that, the gold began to run out.

Filthy Rich

A few lucky prospectors struck it rich. In 1848, John and Daniel Murphy found gold—and plenty of it. By the end of the year, the brothers had made 1.5 million dollars. They made an even bigger fortune from their sawmills and stores, however.

profit: money left over after costs have been paid

Losing Everything

Many people were not so lucky. The gold was already gone by the time many prospectors arrived in California. They did not find gold and strike it rich. Instead, they lost their life savings, their homes and farms, and sometimes their families.

GOING IN TO IT.

MAKING NOTHING.

From Start to Finished

Even the two men who started the Gold Rush did not profit from it! James W. Marshall was never able to claim the land where he first found gold. John A. Sutter was never able to finish building his sawmill without workers to help him.

◀ These four pictures tell a story shared by many prospectors. The men worked hard and made a little money, but often went home with nothing.

▶ Things went from bad to worse for Sutter after his workers left the sawmill. His livestock were stolen and he went bankrupt in 1852.

"What a great **misfortune** was this sudden gold discovery for me! ... Instead of being rich, I am ruined."

John A. Sutter

misfortune: bad luck

Less Gold

As the years went on, it got harder for prospectors to make money. More and more people were fighting over less and less gold. Prospectors stopped pouring into California. By 1855, the Gold Rush had ended.

▼ *The town of Bodie was once home to thousands of prospectors. Today, no one lives in the dusty ghost town.*

Moving On

Some determined prospectors continued to hunt for gold for many years. Big mining companies used machines to find gold deep below the surface. But most prospectors gave up the search. They hung up their picks and shovels and slowly left the gold fields.

Over time, many homes and stores near the gold fields were abandoned. Busy boomtowns such as Bodie, California, became empty **ghost towns**.

ghost towns: towns where people no longer live

After the Gold Rush

Still Growing

After the Gold Rush ended, California continued to grow and **prosper**. Some people moved to San Francisco and other large port cities. Others built farms and ranches throughout the state. The soil was good for growing all kinds of fruits, vegetables, and grains.

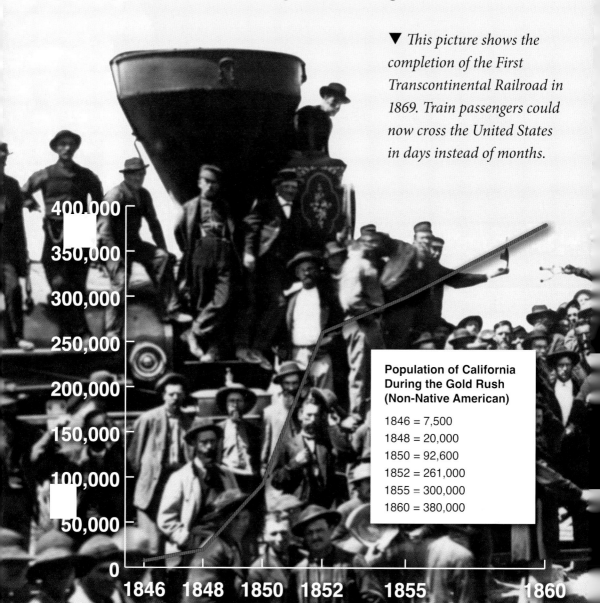

▼ *This picture shows the completion of the First Transcontinental Railroad in 1869. Train passengers could now cross the United States in days instead of months.*

Population of California During the Gold Rush (Non-Native American)

1846 = 7,500
1848 = 20,000
1850 = 92,600
1852 = 261,000
1855 = 300,000
1860 = 380,000

400,000
350,000
300,000
250,000
200,000
150,000
100,000
50,000
0

1846   1848   1850   1852   1855   1860

California joined the Union on September 9, 1850. It became the 31st state of the United States of America. Today, California is called "The Golden State" in honor of its rich history.

Riding the Rails

In 1869, the First Transcontinental Railroad opened for business. The railroad joined California with the rest of the United States. It allowed people and goods to travel quickly and easily across the country. Hundreds of thousands of Americans rode the rails and settled in California. James Polk's dream of a country that stretched from coast to coast had come true.

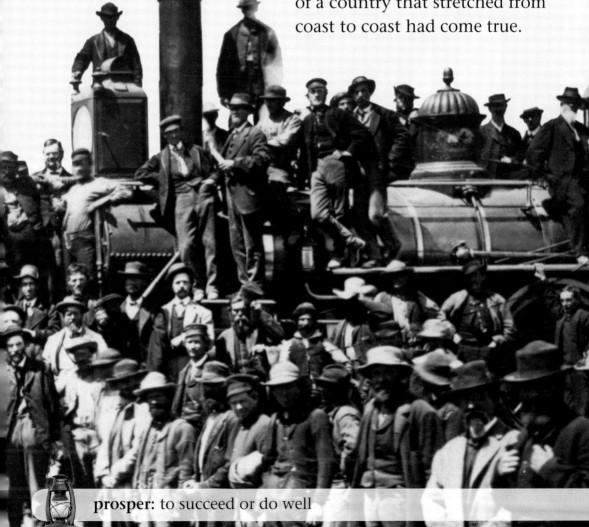

prosper: to succeed or do well

Still Searching

After the California Gold Rush lost steam, prospectors flocked to other gold fields around the world. Gold was discovered in Australia in 1851 and in New Zealand ten years later. Canada's first Gold Rush began in 1858 in British Columbia. Nearly 40 years later, prospectors struck gold in the North once again.

▼ *What would you do for a Klondike bar of gold? These prospectors were willing to scramble up high, snowy mountains.*

The Klondike

In 1896, gold was discovered in the Klondike region of the Yukon, Canada. Soon there was a **stampede**! Eager prospectors quickly rushed north to make their fortunes. Many could not finish the long, hard trip through the snowy mountains. Most who did reach the Klondike did not find gold.

About 100,000 prospectors set out for the Klondike. Fewer than 40,000 reached the gold fields. About 4,000 people struck gold. Only a few prospectors became "Klondike Kings."

stampede: a crowd suddenly rushing in the same direction

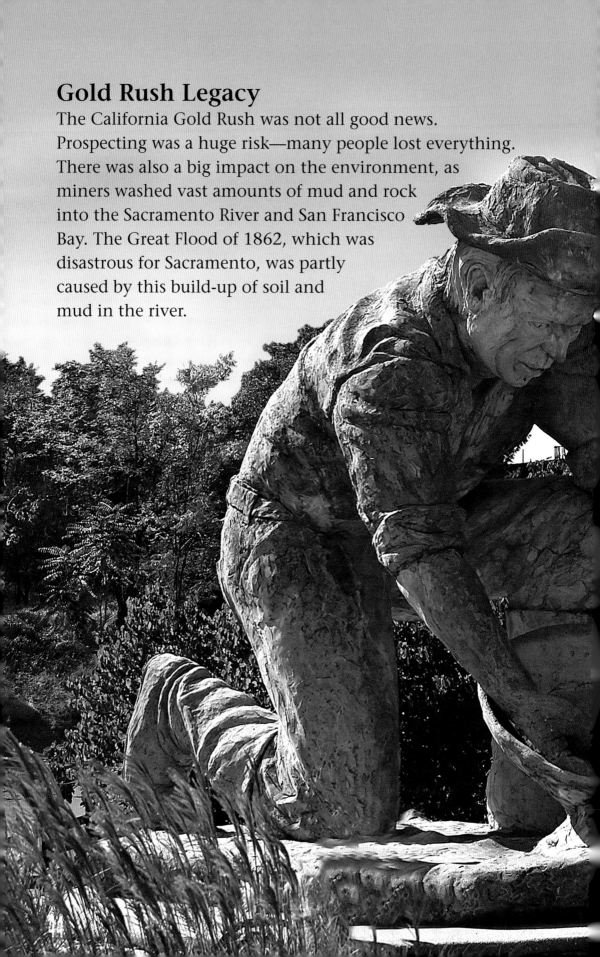

Gold Rush Legacy

The California Gold Rush was not all good news. Prospecting was a huge risk—many people lost everything. There was also a big impact on the environment, as miners washed vast amounts of mud and rock into the Sacramento River and San Francisco Bay. The Great Flood of 1862, which was disastrous for Sacramento, was partly caused by this build-up of soil and mud in the river.

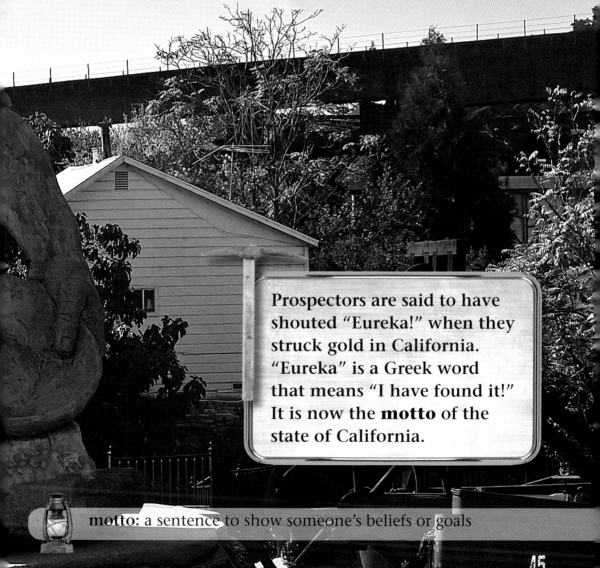

The Golden State

However, the Gold Rush also changed California in a positive way. The state is still seen as a place where dreams can come true. Today, many people move to Hollywood and Los Angeles hoping to become rich and famous in the entertainment industry. Long after the Gold Rush, the state that grew from it is still golden.

THE GREAT SEAL OF THE STATE OF CALIFORNIA

EUREKA

▼ *This statue in Auburn, California, honors the miners who followed their dreams to the gold fields.*

Prospectors are said to have shouted "Eureka!" when they struck gold in California. "Eureka" is a Greek word that means "I have found it!" It is now the **motto** of the state of California.

motto: a sentence to show someone's beliefs or goals

Learning More

Books

Life in the Old West: The Gold Rush
by Bobbie Kalman
(Crabtree Publishing Company, 1999)

The California Gold Rush: An Interactive History Adventure
by Elizabeth Raum
(Capstone Press, 2008)

True Books: The California Gold Rush
by Mel Friedman
(Scholastic, 2010)

What Was the Gold Rush?
by Joan Holub
(Grosset & Dunlap, 2013)

Movies

American Experience: The Gold Rush
A non-fiction PBS film made in 2006.
www.pbs.org/wgbh/amex/ goldrush/index.html

Websites

National Geographic: Gold Fever
http://education.nationalgeographic .com/education/news/gold-fever/ ?ar_a=4

California's Untold Stories: Gold Rush!
http://www.museumca.org/ goldrush/

Huntington Library: Land of Golden Dreams
http://www.huntington.org/ Education/GoldRush/index.html

The Klondike Gold Rush
http://www.tc.gov.yk.ca/archives/ klondike/

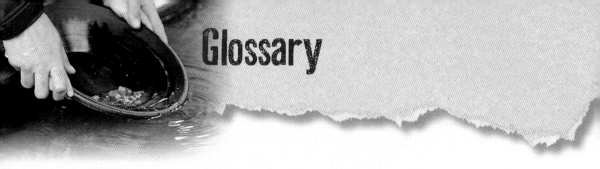

Glossary

abandoned Left behind

boomtowns Towns that grow very fast

ghost towns Towns where people no longer live

Gold Rush When many people hurry to an area that has gold

immigrants People who go to live in a new country

livelihood Making money to pay for basic needs

merchant A person who sells goods to make money

misfortune Bad luck

motto A sentence to show someone's beliefs or goals

panned Used a shallow bowl to separate gold from stones

pioneers People who are among the first to live in a new area

profit Money left over after costs have been paid

prospectors People who search for valuable minerals

prosper To succeed or do well

sawmill A building where logs are cut into boards

shelter A place that gives protection from bad weather

shipwrecks Ships that have crashed or been destroyed at sea

staking claims Using posts to show who owns a piece of land

stampede A crowd suddenly rushing in the same direction

urged Tried hard to convince someone to do something

waded Walked through water

Index

Entries in **bold** refer to pictures